REFOCUS

Starting Over from the Inside Out

Ashley M. Martin

WTL Press

WTL PRESS

Published in Houston, Texas, by WTL Press. Books may be purchased in bulk for educational, business, fund-raising, or sales promotional use. For more information, please e-mail info@iamashleym.com.

Library of Congress has cataloged this edition as follows: ReFocus: Starting Over from the Inside Out/ Ashley Martin

Library of Congress Control Number: 2017908814
ISBN: 978-0-9907701-2-1 (13 digit)
Printed in the United States of America

This book is dedicated to...

The wounded warriors who were brave enough to stand on the battlefield of life. Your silent and loud sacrifices have not gone unnoticed.

The strong survivors who are now thriving. You made it so that someone else can make it. Your fight, your struggle, and your courage are not in vain.

The dreamers, doers, and executors. Keep dreaming, keep doing, and keep executing.

GRATITUDE

My gratitude is extended to...

The Father for His sweet and amazing grace. Jesus for His sacrafice. Holy Spirit for always leading and guiding me.

The brave souls, confident comrades, advisors, and counselors who spoke life, gave wise counsel and helped me start over.

CONTENTS

INTRODUCTION

Refocus: to focus again or in a different way; to focus anew.

Ouch! That hurt. At some point in time, we have all experienced pain points, sore spots, traumatic events, or tender moments. The relationship that didn't work out. The job that fell through. The betrayal. The unexpected loss. The surprising accident. You may still be feeling the tenderness from those painful experiences. If this is your truth, do not fret. You are not alone; a vast number of people are still suffering out loud and in silence. Yet, while pain is inevitable for us all, suffering is optional.

Sometimes, we mask pain by jumping into new relationships, addictions, overcompensation with work, goal setting, or even denial. The downside is that so many have grown accustomed to functioning in pain, but pain is not a lifestyle. The upside is that there are ways to process and heal from your pain.

Let me repeat. Pain is not a lifestyle. While there are painful moments in life, there are things that can be done to help us process hurt and walk in healing.

Like you, I am no stranger to pain points. I have experienced some devastating distractions and pain points – #metoo, workplace adversity, heartaches from deep relationship woes, and church hurt. I know what it feels like to be violated and have my privacy taken advantage of. I understand unfair treatment simply because of who I am and what I look like. I get what it is like to be betrayed after investing loyalty into someone. I know what it's like to overcome deception and distraction. I also know what it's like to make mistakes, get back up, and start over again.

While it was no easy task, my ability to walk in freedom from hurt came when I took the time to press pause, reset, and refocus. Pressing the pause and reset button in your life is a must for the pain to be dealt with.

One time, I was walking on top of some gravel and a small rock got inside my shoe. To my dismay, that little rock was extremely irritating. I tried to tough it out but the longer it remained, the more painful it got. I stopped to take off my shoe, and get that rock out. After it was out, I was relieved. What little rocks in your heart are irritat
ing you and causing pain? What in your life would be better if you just stopped and dealt with it?

Sometimes, although we may not want to, we are forced to start over. Have you ever reset your cell phone? When our smartphones are acting up because of different glitches and bugs, we have the option to reset the network settings or even update our phones to fix these issues. Likewise, when we go through life's difficulties or traumatic experiences, it is vital to take the necessary steps to reset our emotions and mindsets but most importantly, our hearts.

After taking the time to submit to the process of healing and recovery after each pain point but, especially this last pain point, I came to realize that what initially appeared to be setbacks were ultimately blessings in disguise. I admit, on some occasions, I made bad judgment calls. I have learned that all things do work together for our good. We just have to commit to the process.

We often hear stories of tragedy followed by great triumph. Case in point – Lisa went through hell on her job. James went through a shipwreck in his marriage. Gina and Tony, loyal and dedicated, left the group. One year later, Lisa has her own company and is ruling her world. James is now in a new relationship and happy. Gina and Tony started their own organization. Rarely do we hear about what happened in the middle or more importantly, on the inside for them to reach that point.

The real work is done on the inside, in the heart and mind.

Equally true is that from the inside, the ugly stuff comes out. On the inside is where you must reflect on what went wrong and assess what you need to take ownership of. On the inside is where you learn how to cope or process your pain and walk in forgiveness so that you can be free.

Dealing with hurt can cause situations to seem surreal. Not only because of what happens but also because of who hurt you. You never expected your friend, loved one, or colleague to hurt you.

In life, although we cannot plan for everything, we certainly do not plan for pain. Abuse, betrayal, divorce, death, adultery, abandonment, character assassination, mistakes, eating disorders, persecution, and depression are not included in our projections.

As you digest the contents of this book, honestly ask yourself these questions – where do you see yourself? Where do you hurt? Where are you feeling betrayed? Where have you felt heartache, mistreatment, confusion or misunderstanding?

We never know why we get dealt the hand we do but it is important that we know how to play it. The reality is while reaping and sowing is a real principle, there are times when unfair situations happen. Bad things can happen to good people. You may be thinking but I am a good person, not perfect but I do my best to treat people right. I get it 100 %. While all things that happen to us or that we allow may not be good, there is good that can come out of it.

Consider Job, the biblical character. He was a righteous man. He was faithful; yet, he lost so much - his family, his career, his health. However, after these difficult tests and trials, he was rewarded with double for everything he lost. You may not understand it now (I know I didn't when I was going through my own tests) but the pain you feel or have felt cannot compare to the joy that is coming your way if you choose to commit to the process of healing.

Why This Is Important

Human beings – we are all flawed creatures with histories, complexities, and idiosyncrasies that make up who we are and influence why we do what we do. Despite it all, some of the most important things in life are the hearts of people. There is an urgent need to stop the cycles of hurt and pain.

After coming out of a life challenge that rocked my entire world, I took a much- needed get-a-way that allowed me to refocus. For various reasons I cannot go into the details nor should I go into the details. I also believe that there are times when revisiting a traumatic place too often does more harm than good. Your focus should be on moving forward, but you have to deal with it. I cannot stress the importance of retreating from your normal environment for a period of time to gain clarity after you've dealt with heartache.

It was on that trip I was able to recoup, get clarity, and find the strength to face what was about to be my new normal. During that time, I received revelation thatI was just traveling a new path being paved for my destiny and I was truly being positioned for a life of greater purpose. I was being redirected to the life for which I was created and had on my vision board. I was being positioned for the promises I always kept hidden in my heart – greater freedom, greater finances, better relationships, and an adventurous future. I was being positioned to help whomever needs to read this. Because the process hurt so badly, it took some time for me to realize this.

In spite of the pain, emotional heaviness, and mental exhaustion I had after the devastation, I was determined not to let it stop me from moving forward to a fulfilling life. Fully convinced that all things were going to work together for my good as I had been taught, I did my work to heal and began to look at things differently. I did my part and allowed God to do the rest.

My entire perspective on life and my outlook have changed. Now, I completely understand the sentiments of the old adage, “When life gives you lemons, make lemonade.” I chose to make lemonade from the lemons I was handed. My experiences have left no doubt in my mind that if you commit to the process, you will heal.

The question you may ask is how I got there. How did I get on the path to healing and being whole? How do I walk in freedom? How do you get to the point of not looking like what you went through? Some of the answers to those questions lie in the pages of this book. Some of the answers lie within the discoveries you will find once you commit to going through the process, digging deep, and doing the work.

As a wise woman once told me, forgiveness begins as a choice first and then it is truly a process. If it does not come easily to you, you can do the work to forgive people who have hurt you. You can allow God to complete the work. You can forgive yourself for the mistakes you made. Allow the information to shift and reprogram your heart and mind.

I hope it gives you the courage needed to find a new beginning, a message in what appears to be a mess, and an amazing victory story. I believe in you and know you can refocus and embrace any new direction life takes you – even the ones you did not anticipate.

In addition to life sending people to push you into your destiny, pain teaches other lessons. It will expose those who do not have your best interest in mind and those who do. It will reveal your strengths and expose your vulnerabilities. It will also reveal and be a simple, yet, important reminder of your humanity and of the humanity of others. It may be painful and ugly, but ultimately, it can be used as a part of the plan and for your purpose.

This book is not for everyone; rather it's for the dreamer, warrior, and survivor who is here, showing up, perhaps struggling, but wants to get back into the game of life to live fully, love freely, and lead an overall healthy life.
It is for those who have hurt others – intentionally or unintentionally – and want to start over. Those who have found themselves in the midst of a new beginning – the loss of a relationship, a career transition, or a new life circumstance.

The first section outlines the inside work that must be done in processing pain. These areas focus on the heart, the head, and strategies to release hurt. The latter section provides some tools for the outside work – your hands and what action can be taken to start over.

My hope is that it helps you avoid some situations and inspires you to push through in spite of what you feel. Feelings can be fickle and should not always govern your decisions.

As you continue to read, consider how you can apply the lessons I learned to your growth and recovery. Always remember that information without application is useless. I hope you find something of substance in these pages to chew on, digest, and apply to your life or situations.

No matter what distractions you survived, challenges you have faced, or pain you have endured know that you can overcome them, you can heal, and you can refocus from the inside out.

CHAPTER 1

Your Head, Hands, & Heart - Why You Need to Process Your Pain

Dealing with life's challenges impacts major areas in your life. Your head (mindset), your heart (attitude), and hands (actions) are affected in some way. Evaluating your experiences is a priceless exercise and a must-do. After pain or trauma, do not go through the motions of life without taking time to reflect and make changes.

When we experience unfair things, we often feel like no one can relate. This usually happens because we try to hide our pain or stuff it. That is neither healthy nor a good coping mechanism. Please try to avoid becoming a stuffer.

Stuffing is when we push the pain down in our minds and hearts and try to "forget" what happened as opposed to processing it. Stuffing complicates things for you and others; furthermore, it delays your healing. While it may appear to be a great temporary fix, it is detrimental in the long run. Eventually, that pain will manifest itself in some other area or at some other time. At worst, it may erupt at the wrong time and in the wrong space. Dealing with the pain as quickly as you can is the best way to go about getting healed and refocused.

Unprocessed pain leaves scars on your heart that cloud your perspective. It causes you to look at everyone and every relationship through rose-colored lenses, instead of clear ones.

Hurt people hurt people. Broken people break people, but healed people heal people. Whole people help people. It is as simple as that. I have been on both sides of that coin. Being intentional about taking time to let your mind, heart, and emotions heal and recover from trauma is a necessity.

Never be ashamed of your pain. Shame is a silent killer of recovery and healing. Truth be told, society has not equipped us adequately to deal with shame. This is why I am grateful for the work of Brene Brown and others who openly discuss the damaging and unfruitful effects shame has on society. Shame has robbed many people of their complete recovery from traumas, difficulties, and disappointments.

As Brene states, “Shame is the intensely painful feeling or experience of believing that we are flawed and therefore unworthy of love and belonging.” It is that thing that tells you to hide, cover, and not to reveal what you experienced or are experiencing. Shame makes you feel inadequate, depressed, and unworthy of love or belonging.

Sometimes people say, "shame on you" when you may have made a mistake, endured an awful reality, or gone through a challenge. Well, I would like to tell you today, "shame off you." This is NOT something you should be feeling or something you should be wearing. Unprocessed pain and shame attacks your emotions, which can result in bitterness. Once bitterness sets in, it takes an arduous process to excavate.

Getting to the root of the matter is essential. Just as a weed regrows in a garden, if the roots are not pulled up, they will grow back. This is true of the hurts and pain you have buried inside. If you only nip at the surface, you run the risk of reliving the pain you experienced when it resurfaces. Every time you have a trigger, or something that sets off a flashback or memory, it brings you back to that bad or traumatic experience. Triggers are extremely personal and different for all of us. Dig deep friend and get to the root and start pulling out the pain.

Unprocessed pain is costly and can adversely affect your physical health. In the article, "What Does Heartbreak Do to Your Health?" Anna Schaefer reports the common effects of heartbreak include overeating or loss of appetite, weight loss or gain, lack of motivation, headaches, and a general sense of not feeling well. In addition to these and bitterness, pain can manifest unhealthy emotions like resentment, anger, or depression if not properly processed.

The deadweight of hurt and pain bottled up inside will impact you adversely. During and after recovery from trauma, it is a good idea to assess or reassess your health and wellness holistically. It will do wonders for you in the short and long run.

Complete healing and wholeness addresses your mind, body, spirit, and soul. I started a wellness regimen that accelerated my healing in tremendous ways. If you're curious about my journey, I went through a wellness jump-start program that held me accountable for cutting out unhealthy foods, eating a balanced diet, and adopting a healthier, more positive lifestyle. I also implemented a more tailored, consistent exercise regimen along with becoming more mindful of my associations. Pay attention and be mindful of who and what you listen to and allow to speak into your situation and life. If you are around negativity, naysayers, abusers, or doubters, it will delay your healing process.

Embracing health and wholeness holistically resulted in some obvious benefits – losing weight, more energy, and increased productivity. I know the change in my diet and habits had a lot to with this, but I do believe that working through the pain and releasing the offenses helped tremendously.

If you are serious about starting over from the inside out, it may require that you sacrifice and cut some unhealthy choices in food and even relationships. Aim for a wholesome, clean diet, healthy mindset, and a good circle of support.

CHAPTER 2

Matters of the Heart

Proverbs 4:23 tells us to "guard your heart will all diligence for out of it flows the issues of life." The heart is our lighthouse. It is the seat of our attitudes, wills, and emotions. It holds our motives, intentions, and judgments. It affects our conduct and behaviors. The heart is essential to our well-being and impacts our decision making. Your heart – physically and metaphorically – is one of the most important parts of your body and is your HUB. Its health is a top priority.

There are many reasons why people hurt each other, but not all of it is intentional. Again, we humans are flawed, imperfect, and bound to wound each other, many times, not on purpose. These sporadic incidents may occur for different reasons and in different seasons.

However, there are times when people hurt others intentionally or frankly causing pain has become a part of a person's character and nature. I believe people who deliberately hurt, bully or mistreat others are aching for relief from misery or pain themselves. Unchecked and unprocessed pain manifests itself in many spaces in people's lives but ultimately, it takes up residence in the heart. Hurt or anger that has not been dealt with can result in several heart conditions – a hurting heart, a broken heart, a bleeding heart, or a hardened heart

Hurting hearts are on the low end of the pain threshold. These hearts have experienced some pain and are tender with certain triggers. This can be seen in a person who has been impacted by some bad news in their own world or in our society in general. It is no uncommon thing to turn on the news and see something heartbreaking or corrupt. Those who have a hurting heart feel the pain but learn how to cope with these realities. They get through the process of responding to their triggers more effectively.

A little higher up on the pain threshold are broken hearts. These hearts are characterized by intense emotional and sometimes physical pain along with a longing for something or someone. Depression and prolonged grief are common manifestations of a broken heart. Do not think it strange if you experience depression after having gone through a setback, disappointment, or loss.

In fact, 6.9 % of adults in the U.S. (16 million) had, at least, one major depressive episode in the past year. Additionally, 18.1% of adults in the U.S. have experienced an anxiety disorder like post-traumatic stress disorder in the past year. There may be many more that have gone unreported.

I recall feeling depressed after recovering from that blow mentioned above. This experience of being depressed was foreign to me. I had never felt such heaviness before and I did not like it. I did not even know what it was until I went to an event and heard the guest speaker talk about her battle with depression. She described the symptoms as a heavy fog over your mind, which sometimes hinders your ability to think or move. She added, it was as if a rain cloud was hovering over you. That is when it clicked, and I was able to prepare in the event this feeling came on me again. Fortunately, it did not last very long.

One of the most effective things I found that helped when I felt depressed was to play praise and worship music. I am sure that any positive music would probably help to get a person in a better mood, but something told me to opt for this music to soothe my soul.

Isaiah 61:3 states:

> ***To appoint unto them that mourn in Zion, to give them beauty for ashes, the oil of joy for mourning, the garment of praise for the spirit of heaviness; that they might be called trees of righteousness, the planting of the Lord, that he might be glorified.***

The garment of praise was the key to removing the spirit of

heaviness or depression.

Depression is known as a medical phenomenon but like most things, it has spiritual roots. When I listened to my favorite praise and worship music and tuned into the lyrics, I felt that depressing spirit lift off me after a few minutes. I encourage you to try it. Expect to feel lighter and freer after putting on the garment of praise. If praise and worship is not your forte, find some positive music that will lift your spirits and get you back in the right headspace.

If you have struggled with depression at any point in time or if you think you have it, the first step to overcoming it is acknowledge it. I am an advocate for counseling and therapy so if you have the resources certainly seek counseling. If you are not able to access counselors, there are many cost-effective ways to overcome depression that include getting fresh air and sunshine, eating healthy, exercising to get your endorphins up, and maintaining proper rest.

Bleeding hearts are a little more serious than hurting and broken hearts. The pain contained in a bleeding heart has a tendency to leak out through one's words and actions (or in some cases, lack of action). Bouts of rage, outbursts, sporadic or triggered breakdowns are all manifestations of a bleeding heart. Bleeding hearts can also be quiet and subtle, leaking out in destructive ways. The consequences are severe; therefore, plugging and stopping the bleeding is a top priority. You should seek counseling to address those deep wounds. Then, follow it up with heart maintenance that is outlined below to complete the healing.

The highest on the pain threshold and perhaps, the most dangerous is the hardened heart. Have you or someone you know ever acted in a way that was extremely cold and callous towards others? Have they appeared to be selfish and preoccupied with themselves when doing something without thinking of the impact on others? Do they just seem numb, have no conscience, or remorse for their actions? If the answer is yes to any of these questions that is a good indicator of hard-heartedness. This is the worst of heart conditions and one that you would not want to live with or experience from others.

There are a variety of solutions to heal these heart conditions, but I believe it certainly starts with processing pain and applying the greatest healing balm, love, as outlined in I Corinthians 13.

> ***Love is patient and kind. Love is not jealous or boastful or proud 5 or rude. It does not demand its own way. It is not irritable, and it keeps no record of being wronged. 6 It does not rejoice about injustice but rejoices whenever the truth wins out. 7 Love never gives up, never loses faith, is always hopeful. And endures through every circumstance (1 Corinthians 13:4-8).***

Love is very important to the hardened heart. In many instances, the reason for the person's cold-heartedness and indifference is the lack of love or the perception of not being loved.

While we cannot control the actions of others, we can correct our own actions and put some measures in place for our own recovery. One simple way to do so is by having a daily heart check.

Heart checks are simple, effective ways to ensure that poison from the pain you experienced does not seep back into your heart. Unresolved pain in your life not only affects your perspective and everything else that is connected to your performance, relationships, and self-esteem. Heart checks are as easy as a few simple questions. Am I at peace with myself and others? Am I angry, irritated, or frustrated with myself or others? Is there anyone I need to forgive? Is there anyone I resent? If you answered yes to any of those questions, you are probably in need of a heart flush or release. In later chapters, you will discover several ways to free yourself.

Using some of these strategies in collaboration with prayer, meditating on scriptures and positive affirmations had a major impact on my own healing from the trauma of assault that took place years ago and other heartache. Key words I depended on included: "Be still and know that I am God" (Psalms 46:10) and, "We know that all things are working together for our good" (Romans 8:28). You may not understand or believe the same way I do but I encourage you to believe in something higher than yourself to anchor yourself to in order to move forward.

Research by Dr. Andrew Newburg confirms that there is a connection between healing and prayer. His research reviewed the brain scans of people in prayer and meditation. He found that when a person engages in prayer, there is increased activity in the frontal lobes and language area of the brain known for becoming activated during conversation. It was reported that the brain praying to God is similar to talking to people, which is therapeutic. You owe it to yourself to commit to prioritizing your heart's health.

CHAPTER 3

Work on your Trust Issues

The same trust that takes a long time to build can be destroyed in seconds. Needless to say, trust is a critical factor in relationships – personal and business. Without it, relationships do not have a leg to stand on. Be mindful that during the process of starting over, you may have to work through some trust issues between you and the offending party (individual, group, or organization) that can develop after pain or disappointment.

If you find this to be the case, it is important to be honest and real with yourself. When you have been hurt or disappointed, especially by those you entrusted something valuable to, there has been a breach. A violation of an unspoken contract has occurred. When trust has been misplaced, it must be restored if both parties desire to do so. However, it will take work and all must proceed with pure intentions and motives. If you know you don't mean well, just leave the other party alone and move on.

An important thing to note is that you must use wisdom and some common sense. Do not let people back into your life who are not supposed to be there. Truth be told, you cannot trust everyone, but you value and cherish those you can.

You should always keep in mind there will be lifers – the people who are around for a lifetime. Others will come and go but their departure is not necessarily a bad thing. They may just have served their purposes and their seasons are up. With this in mind, you should be all the more grateful for those consistent forces in your life.

Anyone exhibiting toxic behavior has to decide to change, even if that person is you. If the other party is not healthy for you, it may be in your best interest to separate yourself. That does not mean you should hold on to any ill feelings. By all means, extend the same forgiveness you would want if you messed up. Forgiveness is important but the decision to restore a relationship is another matter.

Toxic people with no intention to change their ways or get help will hinder you. On the other hand, if there is a relationship you want to give another try, start small in your effort to rebuild trust. It may stretch you, but it is possible. Trust has a tendency to beget trust.

Dealing with new people may be hard at times but let us make an intentional effort to unpack our bags. How often do we make people pay for what others have done? I challenge us all to work intentionally to stop the cycles of pushing away great people, purposeful connections, and exceptional opportunities because of other peoples 'attitudes and actions.

Recommended Reading:

The Speed of Trust by Stephen M.R. Covey

CHAPTER 4

Self- Examination

Checking, or evaluating, yourself and taking ownership of the part, you played is crucial to starting over successfully. Stories and situations can always be seen from various perspectives. Everybody has his or her side of a story. Even if the other party is guilty in your eyes, owning up to what part you played and your response during and after the pain or disappointment is not an option. You must intentionally create time to reflect on what you could have done differently.

Self-examination assists in making sure you do not make the same mistakes going forward. When you see the writing on the wall regarding a person's actions, put something in place to address it. Be proactive. Remain hopeful but also use wisdom and keep your eyes open for the signs. If you discern something is not right, it probably is not. Do your best to take responsibility for yourself. Do what you can to protect yourself and establish some healthy boundaries in your relationships – personal and business.

Checking your character is a huge part of self-examination. Character is currency on earth and in heaven. Your personality, nature, and temperament all count even in the midst of a challenge and when you are starting over. It is easy to point out what others do wrong and extremely justifiable at times, but how often do we look at the person in the mirror? How often do we stop and pause to ask: what did I do wrong or what do I need to do better?

Regardless of what the other parties may be doing or not doing that may have impure motives or intentions, you want to make sure "your side of the street is clean." I dealt with many lies and slander in the midst of some adversity and pain points. I admit I did not always respond the best way when meet with these things. Checking myself in the heat of character and integrity attacks was a big pill to swallow, but God has been faithful to take care of the lies and accusations.

Along the way, trust the principle of reaping and sowing. If you were done wrong, things will be handled. If you are concerned with what people have to say, remember the truth is always revealed and there are times when people just believe what they want to believe. Examine and reflect on what to do, what not to do, how to treat people, and how not to treat people. You cannot control someone else, but you can control yourself. Let's review the following character checks and see if adjustments are needed in your life as you start over.

Got Integrity?

Proverbs 21:3 tells us to do what is right and just is more acceptable to the Lord than sacrifice. Integrity is one of those words we are often reminded of and see everywhere. The Webster Dictionary defines it as an adherence to a code of especially moral or artistic value; an unimpaired condition, and the quality or state of being complete or undivided.

I like to think of integrity as being honest and doing the right thing. Always keep in mind that no one is perfect. You may make mistakes or have lapses in judgment; however, when it is in your power to do so, do the right thing.
I recall a time when without question, I was being discriminated against; all of me wanted to retaliate and go off in that moment. Had I done so, it would have caused more harm than good. In a world that sometimes discourages good character and encourages bad behavior, it may be hard not to stoop to someone's low level. It may also be tempting. However, the best thing to do is to choose the high road and be determined to operate with integrity.

Got Confidentiality?

2 Timothy 2:6 tells us to avoid godless chatter, because those who indulge in it will become increasingly ungodly. Confidentiality is important to not breaking trust.

If someone confides in you, you have an obligation not to break that trust. You should not tell anyone what the person said unless given permission by the individual to do so. This is especially important for leaders, business owners, attorneys, and counselors. People count on you to remain confidential and trustworthy with their sensitive information. Much hurt and heartache could be avoided if we simply learned how and when to hush. There are times when we may have unintentionally spilled the beans. Nonetheless, let's exercise wisdom and discernment when we can.

Got Accountability?

According to Romans 14:12, each of us will give an account of ourselves to God. Accountability starts with you and continues with a partner or group. The makings of a great accountability partner include someone who cares enough to tell the truth, when you are wrong, or when you are headed in the wrong direction. The person should care and love you enough to nudge you on the right path and get you back on track. If you do not have a partner or group, exercise personal accountability with yourself. Hold yourself to a high standard.

Got Humility?

James 4:6 reminds us that God opposes the proud but

shows favor to the humble. Humility is a very important character trait to have throughout your life. It will help you access the grace you need to complete the things you were put on earth to do. For the purposes of this text, humility will be defined as being modest, freedom from arrogance, being able to give up your pride but maintaining your dignity. Humility in action is acknowledging that you matter while keeping in mind that you are no better than the person next to you.

You may feel like you are being crushed when you are going through pain points. In a sense, you are. Your pride and ego are certainly being crushed. In times like these, you simply cannot fathom what has happened and why it is happening. I'm sure we have all been there at some point. The word "pride" often causes people to automatically assume one is being arrogant, but not so. There are many manifestations of pride that have to be combatted in the heart. Some of these include fear, complaining, people-pleasing, seeking control, not asking for help when needed, and being consumed with what others think.

It is not a natural reaction to remain humble in the midst of pain or what we perceive to be an injustice. We want to kick, scream, and shout. I must note, I do believe there are times and places when we should kick, scream, and shout. Some pain simply won't stop until we say ouch, that hurts! We have become so accustomed and conditioned to enduring hardship to a point that is very unhealthy in the long run. Knowing how to respectfully and confidently assert yourself is the key to ensuring your dignity remains intact and you grow through what you have gone through.

These are just a few of the character checks that arise during hard times. Consider these questions. What have you been faced with? What areas of your character have been tested by pain that you have experienced? What are some ways you can address and correct any shortcomings in those areas?

CHAPTER 5

Shift Your Perspectieve & Fail Forward

Shifting perspectives after pain is like shifting gears on a car. After you clear the fog of what took place and shake the shock of your pain point, you can look at things with a clear conscience and through a clearer lens.

After the fog has cleared, ask yourself these questions concerning your pain point. What good came or can come out of the circumstance? What did you lose? What did you gain? What did you learn? How can you help others with what happened to you?

At some point during your recovery process, you may come across feelings of failure. This is normal. Perhaps, you did fail. That, too, is normal and is a part of life's journey. As John Maxwell states, the key is "failing forward" and "failing fast."

Any person who has accomplished something great in life or has overcome difficult odds will tell you that failure is a part of the process. I have made so many mistakes but realized that none of them were in vain. I learned something that helped me in some way. If you realize you have made mistakes along the way, give yourself the grace to learn from them and trust that they will eventually get you where you need to be.

Failure is not final and teaches some valuable lessons that winning cannot. In fact, failure equips you to win. Knowing how to take a loss ensures you have the capacity to handle the win.

Some other nuggets I learned that shifted my perspective and helps to shape my perspective as I move forward are:

•When life releases you from someone or something, do not chase them or it. If it is meant for them to recircle, they will.

•When you recognize an injustice has been committed against you, research and use wisdom in your approach to addressing it.

•Set intentional and healthy boundaries with people in your life, in the workplace, and in other relationships. Robert Townsend's book, *Boundaries*, is an exceptional read for how to establish healthy boundaries in your life.

Recommended Reading:

Failing Forward: Turning Mistakes into Stepping Stones for Success by John Maxwell

Boundaries by Robert Townsend

CHAPTER 6

Let Go Through Forgiveness

The infamous lyrics of the song, "Let It Go" from the Disney film, Frozen, often comes to mind when I think of forgiveness. If you have not seen the movie, Frozen, it is a story of putting an end to an icy spell on a kingdom. Queen Elsa is an abrasive queen with powers that turn objects to ice. She accidentally freezes her kingdom, and the guilt of it pushes her to run away to an isolated place by herself. Her sister, Anna, joins forces with a mountaineer and his sidekick to find the Snow Queen Elsa so that she can undo the spell. During their adventurous encounter and reunion, Queen Elsa accidentally freezes her sister, Anna, and it takes an "act of true love" to melt her. It was not until Elsa embraces her own humanity and cries while hugging her frozen sister that Anna is thawed and brought back to life.

On our healing journeys, it truly takes releasing pain and letting go through forgiveness to unthaw hearts and walk in freedom. We often hold on to hurts and pains like security blankets restricting ourselves. Once free, our hearts, minds, spirits, souls, and emotions can operate from healthy spaces. We will make better decisions and view things differently.

Just as you must be intentional about processing pain, intentionality is required to fully access and walk in forgiveness. A wise woman once said forgiveness starts as a choice. I wholeheartedly agree with her. We must choose to forgive. It is then followed by the process of healing and recovery. It's all a process! In fact, forgiveness is much like the five stages of grieving a loss. You may be thinking how so. Whenever forgiveness is required, there has been some sort of loss. There has been a loss of trust, a loss of hope, a loss of a relationship, and many other losses. When we lose things, we have a tendency to grieve over them. To avoid getting stuck in one of the stages, it is necessary to go through the entire process until the end. The five stages of grief are outlined here.

1st Stage-Denial

In this initial stage, many experience shock and are numbed by loss. Denial is a defensive mechanism at its best to get through the shock of the loss.

2nd Stage-Anger

In this stage, denial disappears, and anger arises. Anger is an emotion marked by strong displeasure and even hostility. Anger indicates your love or care for that person or situation.

3rd Stage-Bargaining

In the bargaining stage, we voice our should haves, would haves, and could haves. The "if I had done this" and "if only I had done that" scream loudly in our heads.

4th Stage-Depression

At this stage, the reality of the situation sits inside on a deeper level. An overwhelming and intense fog of sadness clouds your judgment and vision. It is easy to get stuck here, but so important to fight so you are not stuck.

5th Stage-Acceptance

In this final stage, the reality of the situation is present, and an individual begins to embrace a "new normal." This new normal may be life after the loss of a loved one, life after a career change, or life after a relationship shifts or ends. Individuals actively operate in their change and work to adjust. They are better suited to live and love again.

There is much truth to what many say about forgiveness being about you. As you release others, it releases you to walk freely.

Recommended Reading:

Grief: Living at Peace with Loss by June Hunt

MS ASHLEY M MARTIN

Radical Forgiveness by Colin Tipping

CHAPTER 7

Release Strategies

In the previous chapters, various questions were posed for self-reflection. Self-reflective questions are key to moving forward; however, there is more you need to fully function in freedom.

A few things I have heavily relied on when dealing with life's tough places have been prayer, life coaching, and supportive conversations in safe spaces. After applying what I am sharing with you, my heart began to heal in a magnificent way. I simply share these strategies as a few options to help you. They are not the end all be all, but hopefully, something here will help.

One note of caution as you consider any release strategies – choose a release that is both healthy and productive. Often, people run into the arms of someone they should not or engage in other harmful outlets to numb the pain. This is neither healthy nor beneficial. In the long run, it will only prolong or exasperate your condition. Commit to a safe strategy that will yield the best fruit.

Crying

Tears are therapeutic and one of the most cost-effective ways to release pain. A good cry can work wonders for you. In fact, some research has shown crying to be a fundamental part of the healing process. When a painful memory or trigger creeps up on you, allow the tears to come, instead of suppressing them. Avoiding a release will do more damage than good.

Vulnerability and safety go hand in hand when you are crying. It may seem trivial but this is important. I would also advise being mindful of when and where you cry. Research conducted by Bylsma offered insight about tears and space. She found, "When you cry and who sees you do it appears to make a difference in whether crying helps or hurts your emotional state." She also discovered that "crying was more likely to make people feel better when they had emotional support." Get your tissue, get a good friend, and cry it all out.

Counseling and Support

During and after recovery, it is important to talk to someone who can empathize with you and walk you through the journey to your new normal. The professional help of a licensed counselor, life coach, or spiritual advisor can be extremely beneficial. If you cannot afford to get to a professional in person, modern technology has made access to counseling easier for the average person. Applications like TalkSpace, 7 Cups, and BetterHelp put counseling at your fingertips. Never underestimate the importance of your nearby support system. Recovery is a hard journey to walk alone. You need continued support on your journey to health and wholeness.

Writing and Journaling

Writing is by far one of the best ways to release unresolved pain and one that I highly recommend. Writing is cathartic. It cleanses. It purges.

Writing in a journal is one of the most effective ways to release your feelings and thoughts without harming yourself or others. This simple, yet, effective strategy allows you to properly process the frustration and pain you experience while giving you the liberty to move forward. It may take a few journals to get out your raw feelings and emotions. Nevertheless, you should use as many journals as you need to dump all of your thoughts into. (There is a wonderful journal application called DayOne that I love). Besides just writing unfiltered in a journal, there is a very specific strategy that helped me get to the root of my pain that may also help you see manifested change.

First, identify the emotion or one of the matters at hand that you are wrestling with in the midst of your pain. For example, one of the things I struggled with during my recovery process was that I did not receive an apology for what was done to me. Wrong actions tried to be justified or covered up. You may have been there before. There may be many times when you have to move on without an apology.

Once I identified this issue, I looked deeper and reached far below the surface for the root. Beyond being upset at the lack of remorse for ill actions in many of these situations, I was angry that my feelings were not validated. Consequently, I felt devalued and not adequately vindicated.

In my mind, I was frustrated with the lack of justice. To me, it screamed, "You are not valued." As an African-American female, this was just other instance in history of being devalued. I highlight all of these things to illustrate how deep a matter can go if you truly take time to dig. I am now quite aware of my value and no longer allow others to make me feel less than what I know I am worth.

After I identified the root of the issue, I found a scripture to apply to those feelings. If you do not consider yourself a spiritual person, you can substitute these words for a positive affirmation. I used the scriptures and words to break down the wisdom from them and began to apply it to my life. It was a very practical approach that worked for me and still does. I do my part and God does the rest. It may have the same effective for you. For the feelings described above, I found, used, and applied Psalms 139: 13-14 and Isaiah 50: 8 – 9. Psalm 139: 13- 14 spoke directly to the pain of feeling undervalued. It states:

> ***For You formed my inward parts;***
> ***You covered me in my mother's womb.***
> ***I will praise You,***
> ***for I am fearfully and wonderfully made;***
> ***Marvelous are Your works,***
> ***And that my soul knows very well.***

Isaiah 50: 8-9 spoke directly to the injustice I felt and provided comfort as I healed.

> ***He who vindicates me is near.***
> ***Who then will bring charges against me?***
> ***Let us face each other!***
> ***Who is my accuser?***
> ***Let him confront me!***
> ***It is the Sovereign Lord who helps me.***

I completed this process for every other injustice or pain point I felt. It's a simple process. Identify the issue, find a scripture or passage that speaks directly to overcoming it, meditate on the scripture, and apply it to your life where necessary.

Forgiveness Letters

After you have emptied your frustration out and have gotten to the bottom of the pain, it is now time to get to the business of forgiveness. Clearing your heart and mind of frustration allows for a clear conscience. So now you can think from a healthy perspective about releasing the offending party. Ideally, these letters are something you dispose of and do not send. If you choose to send it, you do so at your own risk. Ensure that you have given much time, thought, and prayer to it. It may do the other party some good to know you have forgiven them, but forgiveness truly is for you.

Perhaps you have you read this and see yourself as the offender, that person who has hurt others and acknowledge the fact that you need to make some things right. Do not worry. The process and path to healing for you is the same. If you are the one in need of forgiveness and want to apologize, please do. Your role in the other person's recovery may be the very thing that speeds up their healing and ability to walk freely. Again, use your best judgement to determine whether it needs to be shared or not. (See disclaimer at the back of the book.) If you do not know where to begin with your writing, consider the forgiveness and apology templates below as a starting point.

Forgiveness Letter Template ©2017. WTL Press.

Dear _________ (person),

I feel ____________ (emotion) at or with you because __________ (action).

Because you are/were my ______________ (relationship), I expected you to________ (expectation).

However, the reality was that you _______________ (action or inaction).

I forgive you (or myself) for ________ (action or inaction).

I release you (or myself) from ______________.

Apology Letter Template ©2017. WTL Press.

Dear __________ (person),

I apologize for _______________ (action or inaction) at or towards you.

I was being __________ (adjective) and acting out of ______________. Please forgive me. I know I let you down because you are/were my ___________________ (relationship). You expected me to ___________ (expectation).

However, the reality was ___________(action or inaction.)

I am so sorry for making you feel _________ (emotion) and for _______________. I hope you find the room in your heart to forgive me.

CHAPTER 8

Maintaining Your Healing

Anytime a person has experienced pain points, it is important to not only process the pain and release it through forgiveness, but also to put measures in place to maintain the healing with the use of coping mechanisms. War veterans, trauma victims, and anyone who has gone through any amount of counseling understand how coping mechanisms work. Coping mechanisms are ways by which external or internal stress is managed.

These skills can be developed and are important during and after recovery. Below are a few ways to help you maintain and manage your health any time you encounter a trigger or simply need to get rid of some stress.

Prayer - By no means should prayer be used only as a way to handle difficult situations mechanism. It is my opinion that you should pray throughout your starting over journey. Research by Margaret Morris confirms that prayer is an effective coping strategy. She studied the impact of prayer as a coping mechanism on African-American women and came to the conclusion that it was, indeed, something that was pertinent to the participant's ability to manage in times of overwhelming, psychological stress. Along with this, prayer as a daily habit helps one to be proactive in dealing with the stresses of life.

Relaxation or Massage - Massage releases toxins and tensions in your body. Likewise, finding relaxing activities can help reduce stress and help you handle difficult situations.

Walking or Outdoor Activity - Fresh air has been proven to help depression and allow the brain to get the much-needed oxygen one needs to concentrate.

Breathing - Taking slow, deep breaths can calm you down. Deep breaths are especially helpful when you feel anxious or nervous.

Humor - Laughter truly is good for the soul and as the good book states, "A merry heart does good like medicine" (Proverbs17:22).

Pain does not just affect your heart and your mind, it eventually impacts your hands and the actions that come from them. It can influence what you do, what you do not do, and how you operate.

In the midst of recovery and healing, you will need the support of those who "get you." Find comrades or people who can help you navigate the new landscape of your new normal – the new relationship, status, occupation, geographic location, or life change.

Consider these practical and reflective questions on how to start over with your hands or actions. Are you ready to move on to the next chapter (relationship, job, or location)? What training – hard skills or soft skills-do you need? Do you need counseling, conflict resolution, coping skills, or other business acumen? What is in your hand that you can use at this moment to help you now?

There are a few other things that are important to starting over, which I mentioned in my other book, *Focus: Productive Leadership in Action*. In the *Smooth Transitions* chapter, key principles were outlined, which I believe fit appropriately. They may benefit and prepare you for your transition or new normal.

If you are starting over in your career and desire to go into business for yourself, I highly recommend the book *My Boss is Me* by Kiki - Lola Odusanya. It is a real conversation about building your own business and it's filled with golden gems about the outside work of becoming your own boss. It also talks about the things you must consider as an entrepreneur.

Recommended Reading:

My Boss is Me by Kiki – Lola Odusanya

CHAPTER 9

Supporting Those in Recovery

Support for those starting over from the inside out is vital to a successful recovery. It is extremely hard if not nearly impossible to start over without the help of a support system. If you have ever been in an emergency room or in a space where medical assistance was given for an accident, you may have seen the triage system that determines the urgency of attention and care that people receive. This system is a great guide for the amount of support a person recovering from emotional pain may need.

Immediate care (red) requires 911 attention. If a person does not receive support as soon as possible, it could be detrimental. These physical injuries include but are not limited to obstructions to the airway, uncontrolled hemorrhaging, head injuries, threatened loss of limbs.

Delayed care is the next level of care (yellow) that requires medical attention within a few hours. Sustained treatment is necessary for injuries such as blunt or penetrating torso injuries, fractures, soft tissue injuries, or survivable burns.

The next stage of care is minimal care (green. It is known as the “walking wounded.” Medical attention is required, but the person is able to get around. These types of injuries include minor lacerations, abrasions, or minor burns. Expectant care (blue) is given to injuries that overwhelm current medical resources at the expense of treating salvageable patients. This does not mean abandonment. The care requires monitoring and comfort. These injuries include those in comas, those without vital signs of life, uncontrolled bleeding, or high-level burns without a reasonable chance for survival.

These levels illustrate serve as general indicators of how to give attention or support to those who have been wounded. For example, if someone you know has experienced a detrimental pain point such as the loss of a loved one or trauma like assault, the attention and care they may initially need could fall into the immediate care zone. You will be the best judge and best able to determine what level of care the person needs. If you do not have the capacity to judge accurately, please make sure you contact someone who does.

There are some other things that you should be mindful of as you assist others in their pursuits to process pain and walk in freedom. Try to decrease or eliminate your judgment of the wounded person. When going through recovery, hurt people do and say things that they would not in their healed state. It is not the easiest thing to accept but important to consider. Again, if you do not have the capacity to support them, the best thing to do is refer them to someone who does.

Another important bit of wisdom I would like to share is the importance of listening well. Listen actively to those who are starting over. People in recovery often need to just some to talk and listen. Many of us are fixers and are conditioned to jump in and start counseling. We should aim to listen first. Sometimes, the best way to help someone start over is to simply allow them to be heard.

CHAPTER 10

Final Thoughts

Life throws us expected and unexpected blows, pain points, and disappointments. It may seem disheartening and insurmountable in the thick of it, but you can overcome. You can walk in victory. I am evidence of this. I am walking in a new level of freedom for myself. I have found forgiveness for others and myself. I no longer carry that pain, shame, or bitterness in my head or heart. I am now on the other side and in a much better place.

It is said, "What does not kill you makes you stronger." Our experiences do just that. If you do your work, you will not only be stronger and wiser but more equipped for your future and destiny.

Your mess can become a message of hope and grace. Your wounds will become wisdom for your journey and tools to help others. Life's distracting detours can become blessings in disguise, and when life aims to distract you, you can always refocus and start over again.

Starting Over Prayer

Dear God,

You see where I have been, what I have experienced, and where I am. Please take away all of the pain. Clear my heart. Clear my mind. Give me the strength to forgive those who hurt me. Give me the strength to forgive myself. Help me to choose to forgive and maintain forgiveness for myself and others. Help me to always choose forgiveness and help me to experience a new level of peace, joy, love, and freedom as I walk in forgiveness. Thank you for giving me the grace to start over to live more freely and fully.

Amen.

POWER VERSES

Heart

¬ Do not nurse hatred in your heart for any of your relatives. Confront people directly so you will not be held guilty for their sin (Leviticus 19:17).

¬ Then Hannah prayed: My heart rejoices in the LORD! The LORD has made me strong. Now I have an answer for my enemies; I rejoice because you rescued me (1 Samuel 2:1).

¬ Create in me a clean heart, O God. Renew a loyal spirit within me (Psalm 51:10).

¬ Trust in the LORD with all your heart; do not depend on your own understanding (Proverbs 3:5).

¬ Guard your heart above all else, for it determines the course of your life (Proverbs 4:23).

¬ People may be right in their own eyes, but the LORD examines their heart. (Proverbs 21:2).

¬ Put all your rebellion behind you, and find yourselves a new heart and a new spirit. For why should you die, O people of Israel? (Ezekiel 18:31).

¬ And I will give you a new heart, and I will put a new spirit in you. I will take out your stony, stubborn heart and give you a tender, responsive heart (Ezekiel 36:26).

¬ A good person produces good things from the treasury of a good heart, and an evil person produces evil things from the treasury of an evil heart (Matthew 12:35).

¬ No, a true Jew is one whose heart is right with God. And true circumcision is not merely obeying the letter of the law; rather, it is a change of heart produced by God's Spirit. And a person with a changed heart seeks praise from God, not from people. (Romans 2:29).

¬ Yet God has made everything beautiful for its own time. He has planted eternity in the human heart, but even so, people cannot see the whole scope of God's work from beginning to end (Ecclesiastes 3:10 – 11).

Healing

¬ He heals the broken-hearted and bandages their wounds (Psalm 147:3).

¬ The Lord is near to those who are discouraged; he saves those who have lost all hope (Psalm 34:18).

¬ Neither the world above nor the world below—there is nothing in all creation that will ever be able to separate us from the love of God which is ours through Christ Jesus our Lord (Romans 8:39).

¬ Then they cried to the LORD in their trouble, and he saved them from their distress. He sent forth his word and healed them; he rescued them from the grave. Let them give thanks to the LORD for his unfailing love and his wonderful deeds for men (Psalm 107:19 – 20).

¬ He said to her, Daughter, your faith has healed you. Go in peace and be freed from your suffering (Mark 5:34).

Mind

¬ But you should keep a clear mind in every situation. Don't be afraid of suffering for the Lord. Work at telling others the Good News, and fully carry out the ministry God has given you (2 Timothy 4:5).

¬ Don't worry about anything; instead, pray about everything. Tell God what you need and thank him for all he has done. 7 Then you will experience God's peace, which exceeds anything we can understand. His peace will guard your hearts and minds as you live in Christ Jesus. And now, dear brothers and sisters, one final thing. Fix your thoughts on what is true, and honorable, and right, and pure, and lovely, and admirable. Think about things that are excellent and worthy of praise (Philippians 4:6-8).

Forgiveness

¬ So they sent this message to Joseph: "Before your father died, he instructed us 17 to say to you: 'Please forgive your brothers for the great wrong they did to you--for their sin in treating you so cruelly.' So, we, the servants of the God of your father, beg you to forgive our sin." When Joseph received the message, he broke down and wept (Genesis 50:17).

¬ But when you are praying, first forgive anyone you are holding a grudge against, so that your Father in heaven will forgive your sins, too (Mark 11:25).

¬ Do not judge others, and you will not be judged. Do not condemn others, or it will all come back against you. Forgive others, and you will be forgiven (Luke 6:37).

¬ So watch yourselves! If another believer sins, rebuke that person; then if there is repentance, forgive (Luke 17:3).

¬ Even if that person wrongs you seven times a day and each time turns again and asks forgiveness, you must forgive (Luke 17:4).

¬ It was also written that this message would be proclaimed in the authority of his name to all the nations, beginning in Jerusalem: There is forgiveness of sins for all who repent (Luke 24:27).

¬ If you forgive those who sin against you, your heavenly Father will forgive you (Matthew 6:14).

¬ Brothers, listen! We are here to proclaim that through this man Jesus there is forgiveness for your sins (Acts 13:38).

¬ You have come to Jesus, the one who mediates the new covenant between God and people, and to the sprinkled blood, which speaks of forgiveness instead of crying out for vengeance like the blood of Abel (Hebrews 12:24).

¬ You can be sure that whoever brings the sinner back will save that person from death and bring about the forgiveness of many sins (James 5:20).

¬ For the LORD delights in his people; he crowns the humble with victory (Psalm 149:4).

Relationships

¬ When arguing with your neighbor, don't betray another person's secret. Others may accuse you of gossip, and you will never regain your good reputation (Proverbs 25:9).

¬ Be still, and know that I am God! I will be honored by every nation. I will be honored throughout the world (Psalm 46:10).

¬ My dear brothers and sisters, be quick to listen, slow to speak, and slow to get angry. (James 1:19)

Reference Page

refocus. (n.d.) *Collins English Dictionary – Complete and Unabridged, 12th Edition 2014*. (1991, 1994, 1998, 2000, 2003, 2006, 2007, 2009, 2011, 2014). Retrieved September 4, 2016 from http://www.thefreedictionary.com/refocus

Morris, Margaret (2002). The Effectiveness of Prayer in Coping: An African American Female Perspective. retrieved from http://citeseerx.ist.psu.edu/viewdoc/download?doi=10.1.1.634.3195&rep=rep1&type=pdf on November 16, 2017.

DISCLAIMER

This book is not intended as a substitute for the medical advice of physicians. The reader should regularly consult a physician in matters relating to his/her health and particularly with respect to any symptoms that may require diagnosis or medical attention.

The information in this book is meant to supplement, not replace, proper psychological training. The author and publisher advises readers to take full responsibility for their safety and know their limits. Before practicing the skills described in this book, be sure that you are ready to implement and do not take risks beyond your level of experience, aptitude, training, and comfort.

ABOUT THE AUTHOR

Ashley M. Martin

Author and speaker, Ashley M. Martin lives by the philosophy that "You learn something new every day." Serving students and adults, Ashley blends her love for educating, encouraging, and empowering others into dynamic conversations, sessions, and speeches. She is on a mission to help others become the best versions of themselves.

Website:www.iamashleym.com
Email: info@iamshleym.com
Connect on Social Media Platforms @ashleym3710

BOOKS BY THIS AUTHOR

Focus: Productive Leadership In Action

Do you struggle with staying on track with your goals? Do you desire to be more productive and get more done? Don't fret, a solution is here. In Focus: Productive Leadership in Action, Ashley Martin outlines the necessity of the ability to focus in order to lead a better life and organization. Using anecdotes from her own life, Ashley provides tips and tools to help you get and stay focused. Topics include: finding your rhythm and flow (work-life balance), gauging your personal work load, living in your sweet spot and learning how to say no. With the power of focus and all that comes with it in your toolkit, a wealth of productivity and success is yours.

Not All Fs Are Bad: Your Faith & Focus

Have you ever failed a test, relationship, or felt like you f---ed up somewhere in life? have you ever gotten frustrated because you could not finish what you started or needed help getting back on track? In Not All Fs are Bad, Ashley M. Martin shares 12 keys that include: Prayer, Obedience, Filtering, Proper Perspective, and more. You can overcome fear, failure, and frustration and run your race successfully.

www.ingramcontent.com/pod-product-compliance
Lightning Source LLC
Chambersburg PA
CBHW060157070426
42447CB00033B/2183
* 9 7 8 0 9 9 0 7 7 0 1 2 1 *